I0813779

To:

From:

Message:

Trusting GOD'S PLAN

CAROLYN LARSEN
& CORI CHEEK

Published by Christian Art Publishers
PostNet Suite # 132, Private Bag X3706, Three Rivers, 1935,
South Africa

© 2024
First edition 2024

Designed by Christian Art Publishers
Cover designed by Christian Art Publishers
Images used under license from Shutterstock.com

Scripture quotations marked NLT are taken from the Holy Bible, New Living Translation, copyright © 1996, 2004, 2015 by Tyndale House Foundation. Used by permission of Tyndale House Publishers, Carol Stream, Illinois 60188. All rights reserved.

Scripture quotations marked NIV are taken from the Holy Bible, New International Version®, NIV® Copyright © 1973, 1978, 1984, 2011 by Biblica, Inc.® Used by permission of Zondervan. All rights reserved worldwide. www.zondervan.com

Scripture quotations marked ESV are taken from the Holy Bible, English Standard Version®. ESV® Text Edition: 2016. Copyright © 2001 by Crossway, a publishing ministry of Good News Publishers. Used by permission. All rights reserved.

Scripture quotations are taken from *The Message*, copyright © 1993, 2002, 2018 by Eugene H. Peterson. Used by permission of NavPress. All rights reserved. Represented by Tyndale House Publishers.

Printed in China

ISBN 978-0-638-00132-7 (Faux Leather)
ISBN 978-0-638-00149-5 (Hardcover)

© All rights reserved. No part of this book may be reproduced in any form without permission in writing from the publisher, except in the case of brief quotations in critical articles or reviews.

25 26 27 28 29 30 31 32 33 34 – 11 10 9 8 7 6 5 4 3 2

Introduction

The woman ate the fruit...

She placed him in a papyrus basket and put it among the reeds along the bank of the Nile...

His brothers stripped him of his robe and threw him in a well...

She went to the well during the heat of the day...

The law of Moses says to stone her...

He took his inheritance and left his father's home...

Then he said to Jesus, "Remember me when You come into Your kingdom..."

He died on the cross...

...and...

A small word. A word we easily overlook. One we are reprimanded for using too often. Yet, none of us really think twice about using it over and over and...

You get it.

It is lowly.

It is simple.

It is seemingly insignificant.

In some ways it is reminiscent of the manger—so unassuming we could skip right over it. There is nothing flashy or even worth our attention.

And yet...it is a simple connector that can change the course of our lives.

It can change the course of humanity.

It can, with a single use, continue the story.

Today we invite you to join us as we "Look for the and..."

We will visit stories both ancient and modern of people looking for the "and."

Praying for the "and." Some of these people will walk by faith and find it. Some will walk in despair and be surprised by it. Some may never witness it. Oh, there will be an "and" but it may be for others to learn from later. None of them could see how God might redeem them. But, God can see the "and" in our story. He has already planned for it.

We pray that you will find these examples of how the "and" in life often follows tough times, showing you God's constant, redeeming, powerful love..."and" you will find the courage, strength, faith and trust in your own souls.

Blessings,
Carolyn Larsen
and
Cori Cheek

Take delight in the LORD,
and He will give you
your *heart's desires.*
Commit everything
you do to the LORD.
Trust Him,
and He will *help you.*

Psalm 37:4-5 NLT

DAY 1

The Beginning and the Ending

God said to the woman, "What is this you have done?" The woman said, "The serpent deceived me, and I ate." ...To the woman He said, "I will make your pains in childbearing very severe; with painful labor you will give birth to children."

Genesis 3:13, 16 NIV

Adam and Eve, alone in the Garden of Eden, were tempted by the serpent and they broke the one rule God had given them—they ate a piece of fruit from the Tree of Life.

The Command. The Fall. All of us can relate to the emotions that Adam and Eve felt in that moment; immense shame, guilt, sadness and anxiety. A desire to reverse time and change their actions.

And…there is *punishment*

God's punishment is brand new, neither Adam nor Eve had experienced it before. Pain? Had Eve ever experienced that word? The anxiety of the unknown and the guilt of the sin must have been almost too much to bear.

God took that moment of anxiety in a garden and turned it into a moment of hope. The very thing that He disciplined Eve with is what would save the world—His Son in the form of a baby.

Mary endured the severe pain in childbirth so that we might all be saved through our punishment.

What a remarkable story of redemption.

DAY 2

Cain Allowed to Live

The Lord *replied, "No, for I will give a sevenfold punishment to anyone who kills you." Then the* Lord *put a mark on Cain to warn anyone who might try to kill him. So Cain left the* Lord*'s presence and settled in the land of Nod, east of Eden.*

Genesis 4:15-16 NLT

Jealousy got the best of Cain. He saw his younger brother, Abel, offer God what the Lord received as an acceptable offering. But God refused Cain's offering. Blinded by jealousy, pride and the lack of understanding, Cain killed his brother.

The first siblings on earth led to the first recorded moment of jealousy which led to the first recorded murder. Then what? God asked Cain what happened to his brother and, taking a page out of his parents' book, Cain lied to God.

And...there is *compassion*

God's punishment for Cain's lies was similar to the punishment his parents had received when they lied to God. He had to leave home and wander in the wilderness. However, Cain knew his sin was worse—it was murder.

Cain's response to God was, "I will be a restless wanderer on the earth, and whoever finds me will kill me."

God compassionately responds by marking Cain so that no one would kill him. He allowed Cain to live. He allowed Cain's family to live. God punished Cain, allowed him life, all the while testifying to the kindness of God.

DAY 3

Men of Action

We can make our plans, but the LORD *determines our steps.*

Proverbs 16:9 NLT

Dream. Beat. Sell. Seduce. Imprison. Interpret. Forget. Summon. Deduce. Promote. Reign. Plead. Trick. Return. Sacrifice. Forgive.

The story of Joseph and his brothers (Genesis 37-50) can be broken down into just verbs. Each action taken by a group or individual influenced the next action which created another and so on. None of the participants knew how their actions were going to move the story forward.

In fact, they were not thinking about the grand story at all. The only common thread that can be found in all these verbs is God. He knew.

And...there is *purpose*

God knew exactly how each of these actions would lead to the next. Each selfish moment. Every sin-covered deed. All the God-honoring actions. There was purpose behind every single one of them. They all led to the "and."

Joseph's brothers had to beat him and sell him in order for him to end up in Egypt. His brothers needed the famine so they would make the journey toward forgiveness.

The difficult and the beautiful all had purpose. Every action was used to help tell the bigger story.

DAY 4

Good from Bad

Three things will last forever—faith, hope, and love—and the greatest of these is love.

1 Corinthians 13:13 NLT

My aging mom lived alone seven hours away in another state. There was extended family nearby and they were wonderful. But it was just Mom and me from our core family and her care was my responsibility. Mom had a serious fall, that resulted in a lengthy hospital stay. Surgeries. Infections. More surgeries. I went to be with her and rented a room near the hospital so I could be there if needed. It was hard. It was lonely.

After a couple of weeks, one of my cousins invited me to stay with her about 10 minutes from the hospital. We didn't know each other very well though she had helped Mom on many different occasions and in many different ways.

And...there is *love*

Mom's hospitalization and rehab went on for several weeks and during that time, my cousin and I became good friends. Her care, friendship, conversation and laughter all said...love.

Through a painful situation, I found a "frousin" (friend/cousin). Her love is a wonderful gift that came from a difficult situation.

DAY 5

A Battle in Rebekah's Womb

The two children struggled with each other in her womb. So she went to ask the LORD about it. "Why is this happening to me?" she asked.

Genesis 25:22 NLT

Rebekah was barren but her husband, Isaac, prayed for God to give them a child. The Lord heard his prayer and Rebekah became pregnant with twins. The babies fought constantly in her womb and she asked God why this was happening. His response probably did not calm her heart:

> "The sons in your womb will become two nations. From the very beginning, the two nations will be rivals. One nation will be stronger than the other; and your older son will serve your younger son." (Genesis 25:23 NLT)

And…there is *faith*

A first-time mother is told that her two children are destined to be at odds. The dreams she had for a happy family were gone even before her sons were born. Hopes for family dinners or moments of laughter were quickly extinguished. She and Isaac had waited so long for a child and the Lord heard their prayer but not in the way she had hoped. God gave them children but not a family.

But Rebekah had seen the Lord's provision throughout her life. So, now she trusted in the Lord's faithfulness. She had to believe that God would use the conflict growing in her womb for His good.

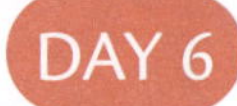

Jacob and Esau Meet

Esau ran to meet Jacob and embraced him; he threw his arms around his neck and kissed him. And they wept.

Genesis 33:4 NIV

Deceit. Anger. Frustration. Selfishness. Separation. The brothers agreed their relationship was broken beyond repair and they went their separate ways. Jacob went to Paddan Aram to live the life that God had promised through his father's lineage.

Esau had been cheated out of this blessing by his brother. He watched as his brother lived out the life that Esau knew should have been his. In his anger, he chose to do the opposite of his father's wishes. The brothers turned their backs on each other and embarked on their own journeys.

And…there is forgiveness

Their individual roads eventually led them back to each other. Not knowing how the other would react, they made preparations to defend themselves when they saw each other. After all, their last time together didn't end on the best of terms.

Now, time had passed and decisions had been made. Families had grown and hardships had come and gone. Perhaps, because of all those things, these brothers learned the importance of reconciliation.

Their forgiveness can be seen in four small words: ran, embraced, kissed, and wept. That was all they needed to go from backs turned against each other to a renewed family relationship.

DAY 7

Just Trust

If we look forward to something we don't yet have, we must wait patiently and confidently.

Romans 8:25 NLT

There's a saying that says a mother is only as happy as her unhappiest child. It's often true. A woman's son experienced a broken engagement. It wasn't just broken, but was a nasty breakup with a lot of vicious ugliness thrown at him. The young man sank into a deep depression.

Understandably his mother was quite concerned about him. She begged God to lift him out of the depression. She asked God to mend the broken relationship and heal the deep hurts.

Over and over, she begged God to fix things. Yet, there was no positive movement.

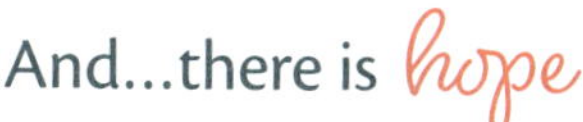

And…there is *hope*

Until early one morning. The worried mother was on a road trip. Alone in her car, she once again tearfully begged God to do something.

Suddenly she heard a voice. Was it audible or only in her mind? She wasn't actually sure and…it didn't really matter because the voice said, "Trust Me. This is just step one."

God always sees what's going on and he has a plan. Never give up on Him. Never give up hope.

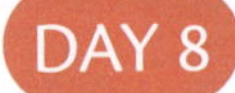

DAY 8

Joseph's Life Is Spared

"Instead of hurting him, let's sell him to those Ishmaelite traders. After all, he is our brother—our own flesh and blood!" And his brothers agreed.

Genesis 37:27 NLT

Joseph was clearly the favorite son of his father. He certainly didn't help the relationship with his jealous brothers when two different times he told them his dreams about their sheaves of grain bowing before his. He also told them how the sun, moon and eleven stars all bowed down before him.

As if that wasn't enough, he told his brothers that one day he would rule over them while wearing a colorful robe given to him by their father.

It's no wonder his brothers plotted to tear his robe, beat him and throw his body into a well.

And…there is *greed*

It isn't every day that a negative emotion like greed can actually save someone's life. But that was the case for Joseph. His brothers went from envy to rage to revenge to greed and that progression saved Joseph's life.

When they saw the Ishmaelites coming down the road, Judah suggested that they sell Joseph into slavery instead of killing him.

Just like that, the stage is set for the rest of Joseph's story. God used the brother's selfish act to put Joseph exactly where God wanted him to be.

DAY 9

Joseph Is Pursued

And though she spoke to Joseph day after day, he refused to go to bed with her or even be with her.

Genesis 39:10 NIV

After Joseph was sold into slavery he was taken to Egypt and bought by Potiphar, one of Pharaoh's officials. Joseph was put in charge of Potiphar's household. He was in charge of everything Potiphar owned. Potiphar's wife took notice of how handsome, strong and wise Joseph was. Every day she would approach Joseph and ask him to lay with her. Day after day she tempted him to sleep with her. Joseph always refused. He was honest and moral. He didn't want to jeopardize his position or lose Potiphar's respect. But Potiphar's wife would not stop pursuing Joseph.

After Joseph's constant rejections, she stole his cloak and went to her husband. She claimed that Joseph had attacked her. Joseph was immediately thrown into prison.

And...there is *respect*

Out of respect for Potiphar and because he honored God, Joseph continually rejected the woman. Even though this meant that he was unfairly punished, Joseph stayed true to himself and to God. He was not willing to compromise his values.

Joseph had seen God bless him even in the midst of betrayal and slavery. He believed that God would continue to protect him as long as he continued to obey.

Joseph the Dreamer

Pharaoh said to Joseph, "Since God has revealed the meaning of the dreams to you, clearly no one else is as intelligent or wise as you are."

Genesis 41:39 NLT

Dreams had consistently caused problems for Joseph. He shared his dreams with his brothers and they sold him into slavery. He interpreted dreams for fellow prison cellmates. They promised to pass on Joseph's name to Pharaoh when they were freed. They didn't.

Two years later Joseph was still in prison when Pharaoh had a dream and called for someone to interpret his dream. Finally, one former prisoner remembered his promise to Joseph. Joseph was summoned before Pharaoh and asked to interpret his dream.

And...there is *fear*

Joseph had experienced God's presence in his life many times. He knew that God was for him. However, could he have been a bit fearful that God was, once again, using dreams as a way to display His power through Joseph? This had never really worked in Joseph's favor.

Time after time he was punished for his own dreams or for interpreting someone else's dreams. And now, God was requiring him to do it for a very powerful man.

Joseph took the opportunity God had placed in front of him and his faithfulness through fear promoted him to a place of power and authority.

DAY 11

Difficult Transitions

The Lord *is close to the brokenhearted; He rescues those whose spirits are crushed.*

Psalm 34:18 NLT

Change may be good but it can also be difficult. Carol and her husband lived in the same city for over 40 years. They raised their children there, made many friends and enjoyed various activities. Life was good. Then their daughter, who lived locally, moved out of state when her husband got a job promotion. Simultaneously COVID-19 changed the world, sending everyone into a lengthy quarantine. The reality of having no family nearby motivated Carol and her husband to move to a new state to be near their son. It seemed like a sensible thing to do but Carol had no idea how difficult it would be to leave everything familiar, including her friends and activities. It was good to be near her son, of course, but she was lonely and found little daily purpose in life without the busyness of being with her friends and many activities.

And...there is comfort

Carol looked for compassion from her family and friends. She wanted someone to notice how unhappy she was. They tried for sure, but they were all busy with their own lives.

From where did comfort come? Jesus. The ultimate Comforter. He reminded her that He does have a purpose for her life. He loves her and has a new plan for her in her new location. His comfort helped her to be patient and anticipate the "what's next" for her life.

DAY 12

Judah Offers Himself

"So please, my lord, let me stay here as a slave instead of the boy, and let the boy return with his brothers."

Genesis 44:33 NLT

You know the story—Joseph's jealous brothers sold him into slavery in Egypt. One brother, Judah, was the driving force behind this plan. His actions must have haunted him when he saw his father's grief...when he thought about what they had done to their own flesh and blood. Later during a famine, Jacob sent his sons to Egypt to purchase food. None of them realized they would be asking their long-lost brother Joseph for food. Joseph recognized them though, and devised a plan to see how evil they were. He sent them home to get the youngest brother, Benjamin. Jacob didn't want to let Benjamin go. He had already lost one son! Judah promised to watch out for Benjamin. But Joseph hid a cup in Benjamin's bag and when it was discovered, he threatened to kill Benjamin.

And…there is *sacrifice*

Judah had carried the burden of guilt long enough. In a moment of personal confession, he offered his life in place of Benjamin's life. Judah had taken one favorite son from his father and would not let that happen again.

He might not be his father's favorite but in this moment, he could be his father's most honorable son. He would willingly give himself as a sacrifice for past sins and for his brother's future.

DAY 13

Lori's Friends Step Up

Let us consider how we may spur one another on toward love and good deeds.

Hebrews 10:24 NIV

More than anything Lori wanted to be on a team in her junior high school. She dreamed of walking up to the sign taped in the window of the cafeteria and seeing her name on the posted team list.

She tried out for everything—basketball, volleyball, cheerleading, dance team and the school musical. She didn't make any of them.

But Lori held out hope that the next try-out would change her status from team hopeful to team member.

And...there is *compassion*

A few of Lori's friends took notice of her persistence. These were girls who were guaranteed to make the various teams, which meant they had no trouble approaching the volleyball coach to plead Lori's case.

Later that week, Lori approached the cafeteria window praying that her name would be on the volleyball team list. Her eyes followed her finger as it moved all the way down the list until it reached the words "Manager: Lori L."

Lori's years of consecutive tryouts could be seen as pathetic or clueless. Her classmates chose to see them as persistent and dedicated. She became part of a team that year where she could put her loyalty and commitment on full display.

DAY 14

Speaking Up Can Bring Justice

One day a petition was presented by the daughters of Zelophehad—Mahlah, Noah, Hoglah, Milcah, and Tirzah… "Why should the name of our father disappear from his clan just because he had no sons? Give us property along with the rest of our relatives."

Numbers 27:1, 4 NLT

Women in biblical times did not have many rights. Culturally they were second-class citizens. When Zelophehad died, his five daughters knew they had a problem. The Israelites were about to enter the Promised Land and Moses would be dividing up the land among the twelve tribes. Each male member of the tribe would be given a portion of land to own.

The daughters of Zelophehad would get…nothing. They were not entitled to inherit what should have been their father's land. These courageous, wise women approached Moses at just the right time and presented the case that they should receive their father's inheritance and thus keep his memory alive.

And...there is *justice*

Moses listened to the sisters. He heard their request and took it to the Lord, asking what he should do. God told him to honor their request and give them the land.

God also told him to tell the people of Israel that from that day on, when a man dies and has no sons, his daughters should receive his inheritance. This changed what had been the custom and gave women a first step to independence.

DAY 15

God Hears Our Prayers

"I will answer them before they even call to Me. While they are still talking about their needs, I will go ahead and answer their prayers!"

Isaiah 65:24 NLT

My job in college was at a hospital nine blocks from my dorm. Bars lined the street between the hospital and my dorm. Bar fights often spilled onto the street. My work schedule ended at 10:00 P.M., just in time to catch the city bus back to school.

One night I was late getting out of work and missed the bus. I stood on the sidewalk debating the wisdom of walking past bar after bar to get back to the dorm. It was after curfew so I couldn't call anyone for help. "God, help me," I prayed.

And...there is *protection*

Thirty miles away a friend was driving home from a meeting when he sensed an urgency that someone was in trouble. He pulled off the highway and frantically searched country roads. Not finding anyone, he stopped and asked God who needed help. My name came to him so right away he prayed for me.

Comparing notes later, we realized it was just at that time a student from my college drove by—also out after curfew because of a delay at his job. He saw me on the sidewalk and offered a ride which I accepted with relief and gratitude. God hears our prayers and sends protection.

DAY 16

Facing Fears with Courage

"Have I not commanded you? Be strong and courageous. Do not be afraid; do not be discouraged, for the LORD your God will be with you wherever you go."

Joshua 1:9 NIV

I'd like to think I'm a courageous risk-taker but in reality, I'm not a brave woman. I don't like heights. I get nervous around people who speak a different language. And most frightfully…I do not like bugs, specifically spiders!

When I was offered the opportunity to speak at a retreat in India, fear leaped into my heart—not fear of public speaking, but pretty much all those other fears…gulp. I had a choice—accept the challenge the Lord presented or…cower into the ordinary.

And...there is *courage*

God would not allow this opportunity to go away. Through the challenges presented in a book I was reading at that very moment, I received the offer for this opportunity and because the Lord gently prodded my heart, I accepted the challenge.

It's no surprise that God was with me every step of the way. I met wonderful women from another country, saw their incredibly powerful faith, communicated with them, tried new foods and even went high up in the Himalayas (OK, that was a little scary).

It was an amazing experience that grew my faith and gave me great appreciation for the faith of people who live in totally different circumstances than I do. God's strength filled me and gave me courage to experience blessings beyond belief.

DAY 17

Remember Jesus

"You have eyes—can't you see? You have ears—can't you hear? Don't you remember anything?"

Mark 8:18 NLT

Life sometimes unexpectedly throws impossible situations at us. Or, we may create our own stressful situations. When life gets messy, what's your reaction? Do you hang on to Jesus for dear life because you know what He is capable of...or do you panic? Jesus' own disciples did the panic thing a time or two. Think about it. They were witnesses to Jesus' miracle of feeding thousands with just five loaves of bread and two fish. A few days later He did it again with a few loaves of bread and some fish and fed over 4,000 people. But one day the disciples hopped in a boat and took off with only one loaf of bread to feed all of them. When they got hungry, did they hold on to Jesus? No, they panicked about the possibility of going hungry, forgetting that Jesus was there.

And...there is *remembrance*

Jesus reminded His friends of the many people He fed from a small supply of food. Two times! And not only did He feed thousands of people, there was lots of food left over both times.

The disciples were nervous about going hungry because they weren't really paying attention. They were forgetting what they had seen Jesus do and then Jesus said..."Remember?"

DAY 18

Abraham's Death

Abraham breathed his last and died in a good old age, an old man and full of years, and was gathered to his people.

Genesis 25:8 ESV

Abraham lived to be 175 years old. Approximately 100 years after God's initial call on his life, Abraham breathed his last. He had lived a good life—a life of obedience to God.

However, his life was not without pain and hardship. God required much of Abraham. His initial instructions to Abraham were to leave his homeland and all that was familiar. Then, God asked him to give the son he had waited years to have as a sacrifice to God.

Next, Abraham pleaded with God to show mercy to the faithful people in Sodom and to not destroy them in His punishment of the evil people there. Abraham followed God's call on his life.

And...there is *faithfulness*

God promised Abraham that he would have a big family—many descendants. But Abraham's wife was barren "and" still he obeyed. His faithfulness led him up a mountain to sacrifice his son "and" still he obeyed. His faithfulness moved him away from many he loved "and" still he obeyed.

At the end of his days he must have been overwhelmed as he reflected on God's faithfulness to him. From a barren womb to sons scattered throughout the lands, God allowed him to live long enough to witness the faithfulness of God's "and."

God Shows Compassion

When God saw what they had done and how they had put a stop to their evil ways, He changed His mind and did not carry out the destruction He had threatened.

Jonah 3:10 NLT

God gave Jonah one job. He told him to go to Nineveh and tell the people to turn from their evil ways or be punished. Jonah didn't want to obey God so he boarded a ship heading in the opposite direction. God knew where he was and sent a storm strong enough to keep the ship from arriving but not strong enough to wreck it. The sailors were frightened and soon realized that Jonah was to blame for the storm. They didn't want to hurt him but they had to save their ship so they threw him overboard.

God sent a big fish to swallow Jonah. He had three days inside the fish to think about his disobedience. Once again he heard God's command and when the fish spat him out, he went straight to Nineveh. God sent Jonah to warn the people of the coming punishment but the people heard Jonah's message and repented so God changed His mind.

And…there is *compassion*

God certainly had valid reasons to punish Jonah and the people of Nineveh. Logically, God would have been justified in wrecking the ship and even killing Jonah. But then there would be no warning to the people of Nineveh. They would have no chance to change their ways.

God's wrath would be warranted. Instead, He showed compassion. He allowed a second chance for Jonah and every citizen in Nineveh.

DAY 20

Participation Counts!

"There's a young boy here with five barley loaves and two fish. But what good is that with this huge crowd?"

John 6:9 NLT

A young boy brought a lunch when he went to hear Jesus teach. More than 5,000 *men* came that day—plus women—and this boy was the *only one* who thought to bring food along. Why? Maybe his mom made him take it. Maybe he had a condition and needed to eat often.

How did the disciples know he had a lunch? Did they canvas the 5,000+ people there? Did God make his lunch known to the disciples? Whatever… the disciples knew he had food and they wanted it. The boy could have refused to share it. He could have tried to sell it, but apparently, he just gave the disciples his lunch.

And...there is *blessing*

Imagine how the boy must have felt when Jesus began breaking the bread and fish into pieces and having His followers pass the food out to the crowd. The bread and fish kept coming and coming.

That young man participated in a miracle by donating a small sack of food. What a blessing! What do you have to give to the Lord—talent, time, money, prayer? Whatever it is, give it to Him and you may participate in a miracle, too!

DAY 21

Mordecai Won't Bow

All the royal officials at the king's gate knelt down and paid honor to Haman, for the king had commanded this concerning him. But Mordecai would not kneel down or pay him honor.

Esther 3:2 NIV

Haman had recently been promoted by King Xerxes to become one of the highest-ranking nobles in the kingdom.

With this honor, the king commanded all other royal officials to bow to Haman. But Mordecai, a Jew, refused to bow to Haman.

Haman, did not take well to this blatant disrespect. He decided to build a gallows 75 feet high and make Mordecai pay with his life for his lack of respect.

And...there is *consistency*

Before Haman was honored by Xerxes, Mordecai had uncovered a plot some men had made to murder the king. When Xerxes heard that nothing had been done to honor Mordecai for saving his life, he instructed Haman to publicly celebrate what Mordecai had done.

Mordecai was a man of honor. He kept his eyes on truth and honesty. He heard of the plot to kill the king and did not hesitate to report it. He was commanded to bow before Haman and would not go against his beliefs. He knew his God was the only one worthy of bowing to.

The integrity that Mordecai showed in revealing the murder plot is the same integrity that would save his life for refusing to bow to Haman. He consistently stood firm in his beliefs and never backed down.

DAY 22

Courage Creates Courage

"Go, gather together all the Jews who are in Susa, and fast for me. Do not eat or drink for three days, night or day. I and my attendants will fast as you do. When this is done, I will go to the king, even though it is against the law. And if I perish, I perish."

Esther 4:16 NIV

Haman was so angry that Mordecai wouldn't bow down to him that he wanted to kill Mordecai. But then he decided that just killing Mordecai wasn't enough. Haman issued an edict to kill all Jewish people in the land. Mordecai called on his cousin Esther who had become King Xerxes's queen to petition the king and save her own people. Esther knew that no one was allowed to approach the king unless he summoned them. Going to the king to ask him to spare her people meant she could be killed. She was looking death squarely in the face.

And...there is *courage*

"If I perish, I perish." Pleading for mercy from the king without being summoned could mean death. Passively sitting by and watching all the Jews be destroyed also meant death since Esther herself was Jewish.

It had taken courage for Esther to move past her orphaned childhood. It took courage for Esther to prepare to be chosen as queen by the king.

Now, it took courage to plead for the lives of her people. Esther's courage led to this moment.

Esther Is Discovered

This man had a very beautiful and lovely young cousin, Hadassah, who was also called Esther. When her father and mother died, Mordecai adopted her into his family and raised her as his own daughter.

Esther 2:7 NLT

Mordecai and the entire Jewish nation were in captivity under King Xerxes. Esther had been orphaned at a young age and her uncle, Mordecai took her in as his own daughter.

Mordecai encouraged Esther to join the competition to become King Xerxes's new queen. The most beautiful women were brought to the king so he could choose one of them. Among the crowd of beautiful girls was Esther.

And...there is *redemption*

Exiled and orphaned. Pain and loss. Mordecai and Esther suffered both. God used those tragic moments as the start of their redemption story.

Mordecai was thrown into a new land against his will. He took on the responsibility of raising Esther because he knew it was the right thing to do. Esther had no control over the circumstances of her life but trusted her cousin to care for her after the loss of her parents. They relied on each other for their survival.

And, ultimately, they both relied on God for the redemption of their situation and the survival of their people.

DAY 24

The Best Second Banana!

Do your best. Work from the heart for your real Master, for God, confident that you'll get paid in full when you come into your inheritance. Keep in mind always that the ultimate Master you're serving is Christ.

Colossians 3:23 THE MESSAGE

Being "second banana" means you play a backup role to the top banana...the most important person in whatever area you are "banana-ing" in. Our culture is derisive of the secondary position. It's made the "second" a subservient and not a necessary position.

Depending on your age you can probably name several well-known second bananas...though not as well-known or well-paid as the top banana in each case. Is being number two always a bad thing? Should you fight to climb over number one?

And...there is *joy in humble service*

John the Baptist knew his position. He was *not* the Messiah. His job was to proclaim the Messiah's coming and prepare the way for Him. He would never become the Messiah himself, but he diligently did the job of preparing the way for Jesus.

John knew his position...his calling...and he pursued it with intentionality and joy. Pay attention to what God calls you to do and be. Don't argue for a different position. If you're called to be a second banana, *be the best second banana ever*!

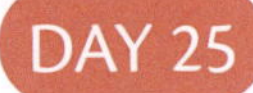

DAY 25

You Are Loved

God told them, "I've never quit loving you and never will. Expect love, love, and more love!"

Jeremiah 31:3 The Message

Satan tricks you into looking at other people and comparing yourself to them. He points out the financially successful who have great power and influence; or the talented and successful in the arts.

Then, he might show you seemingly perfect families where there is no strife or tension. Of course, he will show you spiritual folk who lead with great compassion and empathy, making a mark for God in the world.

He will try to convince you that, compared to these people, you are nothing. Why should God care about you?

And...there is *great love*

Jesus told of the shepherd who had 100 sheep. These sheep were his bread and butter. So, when one got lost, of course he went to look for it.

He left 99 sheep alone...vulnerable to enemy attacks or wandering away...alone. Why? Because the one mattered. He had great love for that one lost sheep, just as Jesus does for you.

It doesn't matter how average you think you are. It doesn't matter how unimportant you think you are...you matter to God. He loves you greatly!

DAY 26

Ruth Pledges Allegiance

Ruth replied, "Don't ask me to leave you and turn back. Wherever you go, I will go; wherever you live, I will live. Your people will be my people, and your God will be my God."

Ruth 1:16 NLT

Elimelech, Naomi and their two sons fled to Moab because of a famine in Judah. Unfortunately, Elimelech died soon after arriving there. Naomi was left with two sons to care for. A few years down the road, both boys married Moabite women. About 10 years later, both men died. Now Naomi had no family except two Moabite daughters-in-law. Since the famine in Judah was over, Naomi decided to return to her homeland. She encouraged her daughters-in-law to return to their own families and find new husbands.

Orpah did but Ruth chose to go with Naomi to Bethlehem. She promised to follow Naomi wherever she went and to worship Naomi's God.

And...there is *loyalty*

Did Ruth know that her pledge of "your people will be my people" would come so literally true? Perhaps she meant she would accept Naomi's tribe of people. Maybe she even meant she would take care of her aging mother-in-law.

She didn't know she would meet and marry Naomi's relative Boaz. Ruth's loyalty meant that her life would be centered around caring for her mother-in-law but God blessed Ruth's loyalty with a second chance at happiness—a new marriage and a place in the lineage of Jesus.

DAY 27

Brody Meets His Teacher

Two people are better off than one, for they can help each other succeed. If one person falls, the other can reach out and help. But someone who falls alone is in real trouble.

Ecclesiastes 4:9-10 NLT

Brody's family moved to a new state at the beginning of the COVID-19 quarantine. He said a rushed goodbye to his 5th grade class, so he could say a virtual hello to his new one. He struggled to connect with anyone.

After a month of virtual learning, the school held a "Hello Drive-Through." Mom pulled the car up to the first teacher who screamed out "You must be Brody! Everyone…Brody is coming!" With each teacher he met through the car window, he was greeted with the same enthusiasm. Until finally he came upon his own fifth-grade teacher, "Brody, I think what you are doing is amazing! Stay strong. I am so happy to have you in my class. You're an amazing kid!"

And...there is *belonging*

"Mom," Brody said as they drove away, "leaving my old school was the hardest thing I've ever had to do. But, tonight, I felt seen again." The next day Brody could be heard answering questions and cracking jokes in his virtual classroom.

It's important to note the importance of belonging, of being seen by others. Because a few teachers took time to welcome him, Brody was able to break through his fear and sadness at leaving one classroom and found the courage to make new friends. Once they "saw" him, he became a part of them.

Perspective

The LORD said to her, "My dear Martha, you are worried and upset over all these details! There is only one thing worth being concerned about. Mary has discovered it, and it will not be taken away from her."

Luke 10:41-42 NLT

Mary and Martha were sisters and were friends with Jesus. He often stopped at their house when He passed through their town.

The differences between the sisters became apparent one time when Jesus and His disciples stopped at their house. Martha's main concern was to make a good meal for Jesus and His friends. She was frantically planning, cooking and preparing to serve the meal. On the other hand, Mary had settled herself at the feet of Jesus and was listening to every word He spoke. Martha was understandably frustrated. She even asked Jesus to tell Mary to help her.

And...there is *perspective*

Jesus responded to Martha's request bluntly, but kindly. He simply said that Mary had discovered the most important thing to be concerned about... listening and learning from Him.

It's easy to get caught up in the pressures of life, even in the busyness of doing good things. But nothing should get in the way of listening to Jesus' words and learning how to live, love and behave like Him.

DAY 29

Jude Works Hard

Lazy people want much but get little, but those who work hard will prosper.

Proverbs 13:4 NLT

Jude dreamt of being a great basketball player. Every night he practiced basketball in the drive-way. Before he allowed himself to go inside, he had to complete a routine of making a variety of shots. The hardest part was the last challenge—he had to make five consecutive free throws.

Long after the sun went down and his breath could be seen in the cold night air, Jude worked through his routine. His mother watched from the window as he breezed through the first part. Some nights when he got to the free throws, he made 1-2-3…then missed. He'd try again…1-2-3-4…miss. Each time he retrieved the ball and kept trying until all five free throws were made.

And...there is *dedication*

Then came the semi-final game of a hard-fought tournament. Jude's team was down by 1 with 5 seconds left in the game and Jude was fouled. Confidently, he stepped to the free throw line, bounced the ball three times and took the shot. Swish! Game tied! He had one more free throw to shoot and his team would win.

Jude scanned the crowd, locked eyes with his mom and winked. He was instantly back on that moonlit driveway, cheeks red from the cold. All his preparation was on the line...*and*...swoosh. Jude was dedicated to preparing for that very moment. When it came, he was able to confidently wink to his mom and win the game.

DAY 30

Lori Gets a Part

Encourage each other and build each other up, just as you are already doing.

1 Thessalonians 5:11 NLT

Lori worked very hard to find her place in the difficult middle school years. She tried out for every school sports team but never made one. She tried hard to find a group of friends and something she was good at. Each thing she tried ended with another failure and disappointment. Then her mom invited her to attend a drama conference with Christy, the drama team director of their church. It was a lot of fun and there were some amazing performances. The last day of the conference the final team was preparing to perform when one of their lead performers became ill and couldn't go on. Without hesitation, Christy pulled Lori from her chair and called out, "She can do it!" Lori learned the part in just a few minutes. During the performance, a director from another church whispered to Christy, "She's really good."

And...there is *encouragement*

Christy's encouragement changed the trajectory of Lori's life that day. Lori ended up majoring in Worship Arts in college. She traveled internationally performing and teaching.

One push off a chair and Christy launched Lori into the life she was created for. Christy believed in Lori. She gave her a place to belong. She gave her purpose. She authored her story to read: "I didn't belong *and* then I found the place God created me for."

Impetuous Peter

"Now I say to you that you are Peter (which means 'rock'), and upon this rock I will build My church, and all the powers of hell will not conquer it."

Matthew 16:18 NLT

The Apostle Peter seemed to be a man who sometimes acted impulsively. He felt things deeply and was passionate about those feelings. Many of us can identify with Peter's "acting without thinking" way of doing life. But his passionate, bold actions and words were not always founded in courage and strength.

For example, when soldiers came to the garden to arrest Jesus, Peter boldly drew his sword and lopped off one soldier's ear—an impulsive action meant to protect Jesus. But a few hours later, he vehemently denied even knowing Jesus—to protect himself. What happened to that bold, courageous, passionate man?

And…there is *a second chance*

Peter failed. Apparently, his faith was not nearly as strong as he thought it was. But, his denials didn't mean the end for him. Why? Because Jesus knew his heart.

Yes, Peter messed up but Jesus knew that Peter's desire was to serve Him with a risk-taking faith. He got more chances. In fact, Jesus built His church on Peter's faith!

DAY 32

Helping a Friend

"There is no greater love than to lay down one's life for one's friends."

John 15:13 NLT

Mallory joined a ministry team serving in Australia, far away from her North American home. While on a weekend ministry trip to India, another student seriously injured her eye. The doctor prescribed eye drops that, if used properly, would keep her from losing her eyesight. The problem was that the drops had to be refrigerated and then dripped into her eye every 30 minutes for four consecutive days and nights.

The rest of the team traveled on to their next ministry location while Mallory and the injured student stayed in a hostel in India. The only refrigerator for storing the medication was six flights down from their room. Mallory set her alarm for every 25 minutes. Morning, noon and night she hurried down six flights of stairs, grabbed the drops, hurried back up the six flights, put the drops in, went back down to the refrigerator, and back upstairs for 20 minutes of rest.

And...there is *sacrifice*

For four days Mallory walked down, up, drops in eye, down, up, rest and repeat. She wasn't able to sleep or shower, and she barely had time to eat. She knew if she didn't head down those steps every 25 minutes, her friend would possibly lose sight in her eye.

Through Mallory's faithful sacrifice, her friend's vision was restored. Mallory's own needs faded to the background as she cared for her friend.

DAY 33

Risk-Taking Faith

He said to her, "Daughter, your faith has made you well. Go in peace. Your suffering is over."

Mark 5:34 NLT

Imagine the woman's 12-year struggle with a bleeding issue. Think about what the health issue meant for her. She was considered unclean. If she had a family, there were things she couldn't do for them. She had spent all her money trying to find healing. She was down to her last resort. And it was her best resort.

She crept through the crowd of people following Jesus. This desperate woman had faith so strong that she unwaveringly believed she would be healed if she could just touch the hem of His garment.

And...there is *healing*

She took a chance and pushed her way through the crowd to get close to Jesus. She stretched her hand out and touched Jesus' robe. She immediately felt something change in her body. Then Jesus asked, "Who touched Me?" His disciples were amazed that He would even ask since there were so many people pushing around Him.

The brave woman stepped forward and admitted she had touched Him because she believed it would heal her. Jesus saw her strong, constant faith and yes, she was healed.

Carolyn Prays with Her Brother

From His abundance we have all received one gracious blessing after another.

John 1:16 NLT

At least once a week, Carolyn answered the phone to hear, "Hi, Sis!" She lived a busy life with a husband, children, work and volunteer responsibilities. Her brother, however, lived a lonely, bedridden life due to decades of bad choices and the ravages of a horrible disease. She knew a phone conversation with him would last hours.

One night her brother called and was especially chatty. After a while, she heard the tone in his voice change. He became reflective, remorseful, scared and vulnerable as he talked about their father who had died years earlier.

And...there is *grace*

While Carolyn viewed the lengthy phone conversations as interruptions to her life, it was obvious that her brother considered their conversations as life-giving testaments. She had mindlessly given details about children, church, marriage but at the same time her brother heard details about how God was active in her life.

So, on this night, all the hours she had spent on the phone led to a gift of grace from God when her brother asked if she would pray with him.

Her brother died a few years later and memories of those calls became evidence of God's hand in both of their lives; ensuring that she will be able to hear his, "Hi, Sis," again.

DAY 35

Ask for What You Need

The sun stayed in the middle of the sky, and it did not set as on a normal day. There has never been a day like this one before or since, when the LORD answered such a prayer. Surely the LORD fought for Israel that day!

Joshua 10:13-14 NLT

You just never know what God is going to do. Do you ever wonder if He hears your prayers? Do you doubt whether He will answer? Do you question if He will act? Do you just hope He is paying attention?

Remember the time when Joshua and his Israelite army were fighting their enemies...God's enemies. They fought for a long time. They fought hard. But the battle wasn't won yet and darkness was about to settle over the battlefield. Joshua asked God to make the sun stand still—to leave the daylight so the battle could continue until his army defeated their enemies.

And…there is *response*

Nothing is too hard for God. He answered Joshua's prayer. The sun stood still and the army kept fighting until the battle was won.

Whatever you are up against, pray. Give it to God. Trust Him. God hears. God acts. God moves. He fights for you because you are His!

A Blessed Gift

This same God who takes care of me will supply all your needs from His glorious riches, which have been given to us in Christ Jesus.

Philippians 4:19 NLT

Lori's family had fallen on hard times. She kept this struggle quiet from friends and family as if speaking it aloud made it that much more true.

Every morning, Lori took her two boys for a walk around the block to find some quiet time with the Lord.

As she opened the front door one morning, something bumped her leg. A large plastic container had been purposefully placed in the center of her doorway. Lori lifted the lid to find boxes upon cans upon bags of food for her and her little boys.

And...there is *provision*

Lori never learned who left the generous gift. She wished she had been able to thank this person for the gift that was both physically and spiritually life-giving.

It sounds like such a practical thing to do—share food with someone who needs it. However, this gift didn't just nourish the body, it nourished the soul. This provision showed Lori that God had not left her. He was with her and using other people to prove it.

It was a simple gesture in a situation that felt impossible; but definitely more possible now that she knew she was not going through it alone.

Pray in Faith

We are confident that He hears us whenever we ask for anything that pleases Him. And since we know He hears us when we make our requests, we also know that He will give us what we ask for.

1 John 5:14-15 NLT

God rescued Peter from certain death by sending an angel to break the chains holding him. God blinded the guards who were watching him. God opened the door of the prison and the angel led Peter safely to freedom.

Peter's friends…God's people…were together. They were devotedly praying for God to rescue Peter. They prayed passionately for their friend. Then there was a knock on the door and Peter called to them. A young servant girl named Rhoda recognized Peter's voice and told his praying friends that Peter was at the door. Even though they had been asking God to free Peter, they didn't believe her. No one opened the door!

And…there is *belief*

When you pray, do so believing that God hears and He will answer.

Trust Him. Believe that He has the power and authority to do what you ask.

Trust His decision.

Trust His heart.

Have faith…and check who's at the door.

DAY 38

The Israelites Complain

The LORD Himself will fight for you. Just stay calm.

Exodus 14:14 NLT

The Hebrew people had seen wonderful miracles performed. They had seen the livestock of the Egyptians die while theirs lived. They had experienced light while Egypt was buried in darkness. They had smeared the blood of a lamb on their doorframes instead of wailing at the death of their firstborn children.

They followed a giant pillar of cloud by day and a pillar of fire by night as they marched toward freedom. Even with the repeated wonders, miracles and protection God gave them, the Israelites still complained.

And...there is *doubt*

For over 400 years they were enslaved in Egypt and at the first sign of hardship as they journeyed to freedom, they whined to Moses. They grumbled that he should have left them in Egypt. They even said that being slaves in Egypt was better than dying in the desert. How quickly they forgot all God had done for them.

We do the same sometimes, don't we? Our fear and doubt take over and make the ugliness we were just rescued from somehow look appealing.

Like the Israelites we forget all that God has done. God saved their livestock, gave them light and guided them. Inevitably we will doubt, that doesn't mean we should forget all God has done for us.

Terrible Plagues

The magicians said to Pharaoh, "This is the finger of God." But Pharaoh's heart was hard and he would not listen, just as the Lord *had said.*

Exodus 8:19 NIV

God sent Moses and Aaron to convince Pharaoh to let the Israelite people leave Egypt. Pharaoh refused.

God sent the plague of blood and commanded Pharaoh let His people go. Pharaoh refused.

God sent the plague of frogs and commanded that Pharaoh let His people go. Pharaoh refused.

God sent gnats, flies, death of livestock, boils, hail, locusts and darkness. Pharaoh refused.

Finally, God sent the plague of death on the firstborn.

And...there is *consequence*

There are consequences for our poor choices. God sent ten plagues before Pharaoh finally let the Israelites go. He allowed terrible suffering for thousands of people. He allowed food to be limited, people to become sick, homes to be destroyed and even death. The lives of the Egyptians were directly affected by Pharaoh's choices.

The Israelites's lives were directly affected, too, but in a different way. God spared them from the horrible suffering. Too often we focus on the terrible plagues and not the ten amazing miracles. No darkness fell in Hebrew areas. No Hebrew livestock died. No Hebrew children died. In the end, the Hebrews were free.

Pain and death as consequences can happen by human hands, but freedom as consequences, only God can do that.

DAY 40

Moses Returns to Egypt

The LORD said to Moses, "When you return to Egypt, see that you perform before Pharaoh all the wonders I have given you the power to do. But I will harden his heart so that he will not let the people go."

Exodus 4:21 NLT

God gave specific instructions to Moses about how He would free the Israelites. Moses' role seemed simple enough. He was to return to Egypt and perform the wonders God had shown him for Pharaoh.

In fact, Moses and God had already practiced these wonders together on the mountain. Moses had rehearsed.

And...there is *caution*

There are times when we move forward with a plan though we are uncertain what the outcome will be. This was not the case for Moses. God had already told him what would happen; Pharaoh's heart would be hardened.

Moses had to move his family to Egypt, get an audience with Pharaoh and perform the miracles God had empowered him to do. All the while Moses knew the plan would not work. At least, the easy-sounding plan wouldn't work. God's plan would work. However, it would involve pain and death along with the miracles.

Sometimes our plans work. Sometimes they don't—even if we believe God has directed them. We keep going; knowing that God had planned on that failed outcome all along. His bigger plan will not fail.

Moses Is Qualified

"I know the plans I have for you," says the LORD. "They are plans for good and not for disaster, to give you a future and a hope."

Jeremiah 29:11 NLT

Moses was not raised in a Hebrew home and any training he received in the Jewish religion was done quietly. He was not a natural leader. When God gave him the job of leading the Hebrew people out of Egypt, he asked, "What if they don't believe me?" He did not believe he was an eloquent speaker.

He moaned to the Lord, "I am slow of speech and tongue!" He begged the Lord to find someone else to do the job, "Pardon Your servant, Lord. Please send someone else." With each miraculous solution God provided, Moses found another way to say how unworthy he was for the job. The truth is—he was unworthy.

And...there is *calling*

It didn't matter one bit if Moses was unworthy. It mattered even less that he felt unworthy. God had a plan for how He would take Moses' flaws and turn them into wonders. In fact, God was so confident in His own calling of Moses that He grew angry about Moses' complaining.

Like Moses, we are allowed to feel unworthy. What we aren't allowed to do is hinder God's plan because we're worried about how it will all work or how we will feel doing it.

God's calling on your life means that He has already figured out how He will use your imperfections in miraculous ways.

Moses Sins

"So now, go. I am sending you to Pharaoh to bring My people, the Israelites out of Egypt."

Exodus 3:10 NIV

Moses was raised by the Egyptian pharaoh's daughter who had Moses' birth mother care for him. So, as he grew up, Moses knew that his bloodline was that of a Hebrew slave.

One day he went out to where some Hebrew men were working. He saw an Egyptian beating a Hebrew slave. Perhaps in defense of his people, Moses killed the Egyptian.

When Pharaoh heard about this he tried to have Moses killed.

And…there is *fear*

Moses did what many people would do when they hear someone is trying to kill them…run! He fled to Midian where he got married and became a shepherd. Then on a mountaintop the Lord spoke to Moses through a burning bush. God assigned Moses a huge task—saving God's people.

There's no doubt that Moses had committed one of the greatest and totally irreversible sins… murder. Then he ran and God used that to get him where he needed to be.

Through Moses' fear and God's redemption, the nation of Israel was about to be saved.

DAY 43

Moses Is Put in the River

Then Pharaoh gave this order to all his people, "Every Hebrew boy that is born you must throw into the Nile, but let every girl live."

Exodus 1:22 NLT

The Hebrews were slaves in Egypt. Even in slavery they kept having babies. The Egyptian Pharaoh didn't like that. He was afraid they would soon have more men to be soldiers than Egypt did. So, he ordered the Hebrew midwives to kill all baby boys born to Hebrew women.

But the midwives were God-fearing women. They made the excuse that the Hebrew women were so strong, they gave birth before the midwives even arrived. Pharaoh wouldn't be stopped though. He ordered all his soldiers to throw every Hebrew baby boy into the Nile River. It was around that time that Moses was born.

And…there is *courage*

Moses' mother protected him from the soldiers for a few months. Then she herself put him in the river. She was not following Pharaoh's order but she believed God had big plans for her son.

Safely wrapped in a papyrus basket and camouflaged by the reeds, his mother left him floating in the water. She trusted her courage and defiance of Pharaoh would save her son's life. It did save Moses' life and the lives of many others.

DAY 44

Woman at the Well

"Come and see a Man who told me everything I ever did! Could He possibly be the Messiah?"

John 4:29 NLT

The woman Jesus met at the well in Samaria had a tough life. Just the fact that she came to get water during the hottest part of the day tells you that. She didn't want to be there when others would have been there…or she knew she wasn't welcome.

She had quite an attitude and even argued with Jesus when He told her about living water and began revealing who He was. But He stuck with her and as she began to understand that Jesus was indeed the Messiah, her heart was filled with awe, joy and amazement.

She was a nobody, a social outcast, a woman with little hope for a better life. Yet Jesus took time to talk with her. He revealed who He was. He cared enough to help her understand. He loved her.

She, in turn, shared what she had just discovered with anyone who would listen. She ran into town calling for people to come meet Jesus.

She was so excited about Him that she ran to those who had rejected her and possibly even verbally abused her. Jesus' love for her spilled over to her love for others.

Friends Help a Friend

Some men brought to Him a paralyzed man, lying on a mat. When Jesus saw their faith, He said to the man, "Take heart, son; your sins are forgiven."

Matthew 9:2 NIV

Such a simple story told in one sentence: Men brought a paralyzed man to Jesus and Jesus healed the man.

The only things we know about this man are that he was paralyzed, he had a mat, he had sinned and he had friends.

We know only a few more things about the men that brought him to Jesus. They could walk, lift and carry. They knew about Jesus and they had faith. Neither of these descriptions offers too much character depth. And yet, this story is founded on the character depth of these men.

And...there is *faith*

We are not explicitly told about the relationship between these two parties. We do know these men had a faith in Jesus so deep that it moved Him to heal another person.

What if our faith was that deep on behalf of other people? What if our prayers moved God to do miracles because of how strongly we believe? How many lives could be changed as we focus on others instead of ourselves?

We may be the ones to lift, carry and have a deep enough faith to move God to heal another's life.

DAY 46

Criminal on a Cross

Then he said, "Jesus, remember me when You come into Your kingdom."

Luke 23:42 NLT

Three men hung on three crosses; two criminals and one King of the Jews. Arguably, the most famous death scene in history.

Suddenly a conversation breaks out between all of them. One criminal speaks to Jesus, "Aren't You Christ? Save Yourself!" He uses the same sarcasm and anger as the crowd standing below them.

Then came a voice of penitence from the other criminal: "We deserve this. We did our crimes. This Man is innocent."

And…there is *confession*

One criminal showed contempt while the other confesses. Why does he use his last breath to confess his sins? Perhaps, he felt alone.

In a moment filled with people around him—aware of the ridicule, chaos, and his own pain and fear—did he look down from his cross and realize he was completely alone? Was anyone there to mourn him? Was anyone there to mock him? Was anyone there for him?

Maybe his life flashed before his eyes and he realized all the wrong he had done; more than that, how he had wronged others. He turned his head toward an innocent Man who was giving up His life for the ones screaming for His death.

Who wouldn't want to use their last moments on this earth to confess their sins and live with Him in paradise?

DAY 47

God's Loving Grace

"I have certainly seen the oppression of My people in Egypt. I have heard their cries of distress because of their harsh slave drivers. Yes, I am aware of their suffering. So, I have come down to rescue them from the power of the Egyptians and lead them out of Egypt into their own fertile and spacious land."

Exodus 3:7-8 NLT

The nation of Israel, God's people, seemed to have problem after problem. Sometimes due to their own lack of faith and sometimes at the hands of their enemies.

One time the entire Israelite nation was captured by the Egyptians and forced into slavery. For hundreds of years they were forced to be slaves of the Egyptians, often enduring very harsh treatment. The people cried out to God for their freedom, their rescue, for something!

And...there is *grace*

As He always does, God heard their prayers. In His perfect timing, He answered their prayers, starting with Moses when he was a baby. God saved his life when Pharoah ordered that all the Israelite baby boys be killed.

Then when Moses was a grown man, God sent him to lead the Israelites out of slavery. He did miracle after miracle to get them out of Egypt and to protect them on their journey to their own land.

Never doubt whether God hears your prayers. In His own timing, He will answer and you will be saved by His loving grace.

DAY 48

Peter Walks on Water

Jesus immediately reached out and grabbed him. "You have so little faith," Jesus said. "Why did you doubt Me?"

Matthew 14:31 NLT

Jesus' disciples were in a boat crossing a lake in the middle of the night. Suddenly a violent storm blew up and they were in trouble. In the middle of the crashing waves and rain, they saw a figure walking on top of the water toward them. Terrified, they cried out, "It's a ghost!" But it wasn't a ghost. It was Jesus, coming to help them. Of course, none of them expected Jesus to walk on the water and especially not in the middle of a storm.

Peter, as only Peter could, took this moment of fear and uncertainty and invited himself into it. "Lord, if it's really You, tell me to come to You, walking on the water."

In a way, he seemed to dare Jesus to bring him further into an already dangerous situation. Jesus obliged and Peter got out of the boat. He began walking to Jesus but began to sink when he turned his focus away from Jesus.

And...there is *proof*

We tend to focus on the fact that Peter began to sink when he took his eyes off Jesus. We miss the fact that Peter created this moment with a challenge to Jesus.

How often do we test God? How many times do we ask Him to prove something to us? Then we may take our eyes off God during the very moment we have asked Him to prove He is God.

Immediately, He is there lovingly saving us, proving His love.

Trust God's Plan

"I know the plans I have for you," declares the Lord, "plans to prosper you and not to harm you, plans to give you hope and a future."

Jeremiah 29:11 NIV

Zacchaeus was a hated tax collector. He cheated people to make himself rich. He didn't care about the struggles of the people he cheated.

But for some reason, when he heard that Jesus was coming to town, Zacchaeus wanted to see Him. However, he was a short man, stuck at the back of the crowd. He didn't have a chance of seeing Jesus pass by. No one in the crowd would let him move to the front because they hated him.

And...there is *a plan*

Zacchaeus was an adult—30, 40, 50+ years old. We don't really know his age. We know that he was a cheating tax collector. We know he was hated.

We assume that up until this point in his life, he had no interest in God. But here he is, wanting to see Jesus and wouldn't you know it...there's a tree for him to climb so he can do just that. The tree didn't just pop up. It began growing years before this day.

God planted the tree so on that day Zacchaeus could meet Jesus and have his life forever changed.

Trust God's plan.

DAY 50

Abraham Obeys

At that moment the angel of the LORD called to him from heaven, "Abraham! Abraham!" "Yes," Abraham replied. "Here I am!"

Genesis 22:11 NLT

Abraham and Sarah waited a long, long time to become parents. Then God blessed them with a son whom they named Isaac. They were thrilled!

One day God called Abraham who responded, only to hear the words that must have brought him to his knees. God asked him to sacrifice his son, Isaac. Abraham took Isaac and some servants up a mountain.

Only Abraham knew he was preparing for Isaac's death. God had called Abraham and he answered, "Here I am." He would obey God regardless of how difficult and painful it was.

And…there is *presence*

Abraham placed his son on the altar and raised the knife to sacrifice him, but God called out again. "Here I am," Abraham responded. The last time God called out to him, he was asked to kill his precious son. Why would Abraham answer God's call again? Perhaps because he knew that God was there. God was with him through the preparations, through the moments that Abraham thought would be Isaac's last.

God stopped Abraham from killing his son because he saw Abraham faithfully follow through with His command.

Just like Abraham we are called to listen, to respond, to trust God's presence and goodness in our lives.

DAY 51

Joseph Flees to Egypt

An angel of the Lord appeared to Joseph in a dream. "Get up! Flee to Egypt with the child and his mother," the angel said.

Matthew 2:13 NLT

Almost overnight, Joseph found himself the patriarch of a little family. They relied on him to provide for their needs and their safety.

The last time he had a dream, God revealed that his fiancée was pregnant with the Son of God.

After the Baby was born, Joseph had another dream telling him to take his family to a different country. His dreams brought huge life changes.

And...there is loss

The census forced Joseph and Mary to leave their hometown and go to Bethlehem where Jesus was born. Now, King Herod's jealousy forced them to leave their country and cross the desert into Egypt to protect their infant child.

They had already lost friends, family, jobs, and their home. Now they would be immigrants, potentially losing their heritage, history and even their identities.

They were about to suffer more loss but in that loss, find their safety.

They had to lose many things so that they could save what mattered most: Jesus.

DAY 52

Waiting on God

Be still in the presence of the Lord, *and wait patiently for Him to act.*

Psalm 37:7 NLT

I confess that I am not a patient person. Well, I can be patient waiting for things to happen as long as the end result will be what I want. Yes, I have control issues.

I often read the end of a book before I can handle the crises of the characters. I want to know how a movie ends before I watch it.

When a treasured relationship was fractured, my lack of patience became even more troublesome. I wanted to attack the problem, fix it and get things back to normal. However, every effort toward that end was met with resistance.

And…there is *patience*

The Father had to literally speak into my heart and mind over and over again: "Just stop. Be patient. Quit trying to manipulate things. I have this. I know what I'm doing."

It was hard. Very hard. But, as time went on, I learned that, as much as I wanted the broken to be repaired, I couldn't control it. I learned to be patient by trusting my loving God. He loves me. He loves the other person in this situation, too.

And yes, He knows what He's doing and has only the best outcome planned for us both.

DAY 53

A Change in Zacchaeus

Meanwhile, Zacchaeus stood before the Lord and said, "I will give half my wealth to the poor, Lord, and if I have cheated people on their taxes, I will give them back four times as much!"

Luke 19:8 NLT

As the chief tax collector, Zacchaeus was one of the most despised men in Jericho. We aren't told why Zacchaeus wanted to see Jesus. Perhaps he had heard of Jesus' miracles and was curious.

As someone people disliked and distrusted, it's interesting that Zacchaeus would have any interest in seeing Jesus.

And yet, he went out of his way to set his eyes on Jesus. He climbed up in a tree above everyone else, just to get a look at Him.

And…there is *confession*

Maybe Zacchaeus was just curious; or maybe he was craving the opportunity to confess his sins. There are times when our sins become too much and we seek out an opportunity to come clean.

The Bible says that after Jesus told Zacchaeus to come down from the tree, the tax collector did so quickly and welcomed Jesus to his home.

Perhaps Zacchaeus' heart already felt lighter knowing that he was about to unburden it. He sat down with Jesus and confessed that he had cheated people. He promised to make things right with the poor and those he had cheated. He sought out Jesus and followed through on his confession because he knew he needed to clear the way for the next part of his story.

Is your pathway clear for what God has next for you?

DAY 54

Nebuchadnezzar Turns Up the Heat

Nebuchadnezzar said, "Praise to the God of Shadrach, Meshach, and Abednego! He sent His angel to rescue His servants who trusted in Him. They defied the king's command and were willing to die rather than serve or worship any god except their own God."

Daniel 3:28 NLT

Nebuchadnezzar had a giant statue of himself made and ordered that everyone in his kingdom bow and worship it. Any who disobeyed would be thrown into a fiery furnace.

The proclamation was followed by the people… until Shadrach, Meshach and Abednego refused to obey the king's demands. They told him that they would never obey this command. They would bow only to God in worship.

These three men were confident that God would rescue them, not only from the furnace, but also from King Nebuchadnezzar's power. Essentially, they were saying that his power was useless before their God.

And...there is *salvation*

Nebuchadnezzar's anger allowed for the powerful greatness of God to shine bright—brighter than a furnace heated seven times hotter than before. The king thought he had won. But he was proven wrong. Pride and anger didn't have the last say; it was simply used as a torch to ignite redemption and bring the salvation of three godly men.

DAY 55

Sharon Leaves a Voicemail

Many are the plans in a person's heart, but it is the LORD's purpose that prevails.

Proverbs 19:21 NIV

"Hi, this is Sharon calling again. We would like to schedule an interview for the Office Coordinator position."

Sharon left that voicemail four different times before she finally received a call back.

For a number of reasons, Lori was dealing with a bout of depression and couldn't bring herself to return the call. Even if it was for a good reason.

And...there is *persistence*

Sharon persisted in reaching out to Lori...on Lori's behalf. One follow-up call to an original message is understandable but three follow-up calls? Little did Sharon know that her persistence was about to change Lori's life and future.

Lori finally returned the call and got the job, which equipped her for her career that gave her life-long friends who walked alongside her through some of her darkest days.

Lori's future was shaped by a stranger who, only by the grace of God, did not give up on her.

DAY 56

"Go There!"

Then both Philip and the eunuch went down into the water and Philip baptized him. When they came up out of the water, the Spirit of the Lord suddenly took Philip away, and the eunuch did not see him again, but went on his way rejoicing.

Acts 8:38-39 NIV

Christians were being persecuted. Saul was hunting them down and throwing them in jail, or worse. There was a powerful effort to shut down the growth of the new church.

But those who believed Jesus was the Messiah kept right on preaching about Him. No one was going to stop them.

One believer, a man named Philip, was among those who kept preaching and doing God's work. He was an obedient follower, even in the face of persecution.

And...there is *guidance*

The Holy Spirit gave Philip a direct message telling him what road to travel on and to chase down a chariot he would see on the road.

Was it where Philip had planned to go? It didn't matter. When the Spirit spoke, Philip obeyed.

Because of the Spirit's guidance, Philip was able to explain the gospel to the Ethiopian eunuch and then baptize him as a new believer! Obeying guidance leads to great things!

DAY 57

Lori Is Locked Out

Trust in the Lord *with all your heart; do not depend on your own understanding.*

Proverbs 3:5 NLT

Lori was seven months pregnant with her third son. The daily routine of getting herself and two toddlers out of the house each day felt like an Olympic sport. One morning, after a last check to make sure everyone had pants on, they slammed the door and made their way to the car. Her two little boys stood at the car door shouting for her to unlock it.

Lori reached into her purse for the car keys then realized they were in the house…the locked house. Lori and her boys ran around the house frantically trying to open windows and doors. They were all firmly locked. Feeling defeated, Lori sat down on the porch. Her four-year-old son quietly said, "Mommy, let's pray for God to unlock the door."

And…there is *faith*

Well, while a four-year-old's faith didn't unlock the doors that day, it did unlock Lori's perspective on faith. Why didn't she think to pray for God to miraculously unlock the door?

Too much life had been lived to have that simple, trusting faith of her child.

Her son's faith didn't unlock the doors but it did help unlock Lori's child-like faith.

A Wise Donkey

The Lord opened Balaam's eyes, and he saw the angel of the Lord standing in the roadway with a drawn sword in His hand. Balaam bowed his head and fell face down on the ground before Him.

Numbers 22:31 NLT

Balak, the Moabite king, wanted to hurt God's people. In fact, he asked Balaam, a prophet of God, to put a curse on them.

Of course, God told Balaam not to because He dearly loved His people and they were blessed.

However, Balak was persistent so God allowed Balaam to go hear what the king's plan was. But, God wanted to be sure that Balaam would say only what the Spirit told him to say.

And…there is *protection*

Balaam was riding on a donkey to go to the king. God allowed his donkey to see God's powerful angel standing with sword drawn to stop Balaam from going to Balak.

Three times the donkey ran off the road or bumped Balaam into a wall or simply laid down on the road. Three times Balaam beat his donkey.

Then God allowed the donkey to actually speak and tell Balaam he was seeing God's angel. Finally, God opened Balaam's eyes to the angel.

Balaam discovered that the donkey was actually saving his life because the angel would have killed Balaam to stop him from going to the king. God will go to amazing lengths to protect His people.

DAY 59

Hearing My Name

May you have the power to understand, as all God's people should, how wide, how long, how high, and how deep His love is.

Ephesians 3:18 NLT

For three and a half years my friends and I had prayed for our dear, dear friend Barbara as she fought cancer. However, now Barbara was slipping away from this life. We took turns sitting with her throughout the days and nights, giving her husband an opportunity to rest a bit.

Early one morning, I was sitting beside her bed, knowing that my dear friend would soon leave this life. Exhausted from being there all night, I rested my head on the side of the bed and allowed grief to flood my soul.

Besides being a dear friend, Barbara had been an influential spiritual mentor to me. She had been unresponsive for a few days and I very much wanted to just hear her voice once more.

And...there are *gifts*

In the midst of my sobs, I heard my name. My dear friend was looking at me and had spoken my name...just one time. What a gift our loving Father gave me. One word. My name. Spoken by my friend.

God gave me the gift of this precious memory because His attention to us is constant; His love is deep and He cares about even just the desire to hear a loved one's voice one more time.

DAY 60

Eric Gets a Job

"Ask and it will be given to you; seek and you will find; knock and the door will be opened to you."

Luke 11:9 NIV

Eric spent most of his working career in the telecom industry. As technology changed and advanced, the need for workers with his skills did not. He found himself unemployed in his 50s with a wife and three children.

After three and a half years of searching for a full-time job while working several part-time jobs, he found a position with a missionary organization.

For a few years he dedicated his life to serving those who were serving the Lord overseas. He enjoyed the work very much. Almost without warning, the organization moved across the country. Eric once again found himself unemployed.

On his daily commute to work, he had always passed a Trader Joe's grocery store and when he learned he was about to be unemployed again, on a whim, he stopped and asked if they were hiring. They were not but he was told to check again sometime.

And...there is *persistence*

For almost a year, Eric stopped in at Trader Joe's every Monday to ask if they were hiring. He was never agitated, rude or impatient. He was kind, pleasant and hopeful.

His persistence paid off when the manager offered him a position knowing that this man would be a dedicated and hard worker. He had witnessed that already.

DAY 61

God's Power, Love and Nearness

Blessed be the God and Father of our Lord Jesus Christ, the Father of mercies and God of all comfort, who comforts us in all our affliction, so that we may be able to comfort those who are in any affliction, with the comfort with which we ourselves are comforted by God.

2 Corinthians 1:3-4 ESV

Maybe you know someone who has experienced this…or perhaps you have personally heard the words, "It's cancer." It's hard to hear much else after those two words are delivered. Your mind races to all the "what ifs" and the dread of treatments mixed with the hope that they work for you. Of course, we all realize that we won't get out of this life alive but the reality of knowing something has happened that could mean the end is close, well, that is unnerving.

And...there is *comfort*

In your moments of angst, remember the many, many times Jesus healed the sick, raised the dead and gave sight to the blind as He answered the faith-filled requests for help. Remember when He raised a young man back to life and gave him back to his grief-stricken mother. Remember when God raised Jesus Himself back to life.

Remember three things:

1. God's power is majestic, strong and greater than anything.
2. God loves you more than you can even begin to imagine.
3. You will not take even one step of this journey alone.

DAY 62

Rusty Goes Outside

Don't forget to do good and to share with those in need. These are the sacrifices that please God.

Hebrews 13:16 NLT

Ann was a nurse caring for Rusty as he battled multiple sclerosis. He was bedfast so she came to his home each day to help him. Ann soon noticed a theme in her daily conversations with him. When she walked in the door, Rusty's first questions would be, "What's it like out there today? Is it warm? Is there a breeze? Man, I wish I could feel the sunshine again." Day after day, he asked about the weather, always ending the conversation with an (unconscious) wish to feel the outdoors again.

Within a matter of weeks, Ann came to his house in a pick-up truck carrying the "Rusty Mobile" in the back. She built it from a gurney and a wheelchair. It was hospital bed height so she rolled him over onto the padded top, grabbed the handles and pushed him outside.

And…there is joy

Rusty hadn't felt the breeze in his face or the sun in his eyes for years. The sun shone so brightly that it forced his eyes closed.

Joy welled up from deep in his spirit, curling his lips into the biggest smile Ann had ever seen.

In that moment, Ann's thoughtful creativity provided joy so great even Rusty's MS-fatigued muscles couldn't contain it.

DAY 63

Hagar Is Seen

Then the angel of the Lord told her, "Go back to your mistress and submit to her." The angel added, "I will increase your descendants so much that they will be too numerous to count."

Genesis 16:9-10 NIV

Hagar was a slave woman who was owned by Sarah and Abraham. It must have seemed to her that she was only created for others to use. She had no control of her own life so she did as she was told.

Her owner, Sarah, was unable to become pregnant but she very much wanted a child. As a way to have a family, Sarah offered Hagar to Abraham. It was after being forced into bed with Abraham that Hagar's anger began to surface.

She became pregnant with Abraham's child and despised both Abraham and Sarah because of it. Her daily life, her identity and now her body were all being controlled by Sarah. When Sarah began to mistreat her because she was threatened by Hagar's son being Abraham's heir, Hagar ran away.

And...there is *understanding*

When life became too much, Hagar did the only thing she could think to do...run. The angel of the Lord found where Hagar was hiding and basically said, "I understand. This is awful. Go back to your master and know that I will reward you."

We all want to be understood. We all want to know that the pain and anger we are feeling is valid. We serve a God who not only understands but redeems us as a result of His understanding.

DAY 64

Hagar Is Sent Away

Then God opened her eyes and she saw a well of water. So she went and filled the skin with water and gave the boy a drink.

Genesis 21:19 NIV

Hagar did everything she was told to do but she was still being punished. When Sarah made her sleep with Abraham in order to give him a son, she did it. When she ran away and God told her to go back and serve her mistress, she did it.

Each request and challenge she was presented with, she did. When Sarah conceived a son herself, she felt threatened by Hagar's "lineage-saving" son. Sarah didn't want anything or anyone to come between her son, Isaac, and his inheritance.

So, Sarah insisted that Abraham take Hagar and her son, Ishmael, and leave them in the desert.

And…there is *provision*

Hagar was forced out into the desert with her son. No shelter, no nourishment, no money, no family, no hope.

God met her there. He provided comfort to her emotional needs. He provided water for their physical needs. And, He provided hope for her future needs.

Through His provisions, He promised to make Ishmael into a great nation. God provided for her immediate needs. He also promised to provide for the needs in her future.

DAY 65

Repent and Be Saved

Repent, therefore, of this wickedness of yours, and pray to the Lord that, if possible, the intent of your heart may be forgiven you.

Acts 8:22 ESV

I never thought of myself as a judgmental person—until one Sunday morning worship service. I settled in a pew near the back of the church. The service began and we stood to sing a hymn. That was when I saw a young man near the front. His head was shaved except for a small ponytail at the back. He did not look like someone who belonged in our evangelical church. "What is *he* doing here?" was my first thought and my thoughts and attitude slid downhill from there.

When the song ended, the young man turned to pick something up before he sat down again and I recognized him. He was a young man from our high school youth group who had the lead role in the high school production of *The King and I*.

And...there is *repentance*

I came face to face with my judgmental spirit and I immediately repented, asking God's forgiveness.

What if that had been a young man actively seeking truth, curious about Jesus' love? I learned that day to be more accepting, to realize that "it's the sick who need a doctor" and I should welcome all who come into the church seeking, even if they look different.

Teamwork Victories

When Moses' hands grew tired, they took a stone and put it under him and he sat on it. Aaron and Hur held his hands up—one on one side, one on the other—so that his hands remained steady till sunset.

Exodus 17:12 NIV

Do you rush through life trying to do things on your own, refusing offers of help from others? Do you sometimes fail miserably simply because you do, in fact, need the help you have refused? Does this drive to do everything by yourself make you feel alone and even unappreciated?

Think about Moses. God gave him the job of leading the Israelite nation to freedom. The people moaned and complained throughout the 40 years of traveling to the Promised Land. God did communicate. He spoke directly to Moses who delivered God's messages to the people. Moses certainly had a big responsibility. He did have to do many things alone.

One time the Israelites were attacked by an enemy army. Joshua led the Israelite army into battle. God promised a victory as long as Moses held his shepherd's staff in the air. While his arms were up, the Israelites were defeating their enemy but when his arms dropped the enemy began to win.

And...there is *teamwork*

Aaron and Hur came alongside Moses—one on each side—and they held his arms in the air until the battle was won. Moses needed help and God provided.

Maybe there are times when you need help, too...and God will provide.

DAY 67

Never Give Up Hope

Elisha said, "Here, take your son!" She fell at his feet and bowed before him, overwhelmed with gratitude. Then she took her son in her arms and carried him downstairs.

2 Kings 4:36-37 NLT

The wealthy woman from Shunem was given her heart's desire—a son. That precious gift was in response to her unselfish kindness to God's prophet, Elisha. She and her husband built a room in their home for him to stay in whenever he came to Shunem and she was rewarded with the birth of her son—something she had always wanted.

If you've ever had a life-long desire fulfilled then you know it's humbling, exciting and well, just an incredible blessing. But then, for the Shunammite woman there was heartbreak. Her son…a surprise blessing given…was taken away. Heartbreak. Confusion. Maybe anger. But she didn't give up.

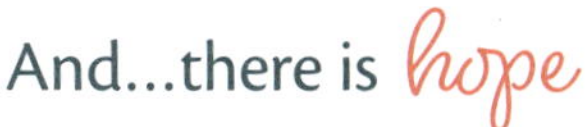

The distraught mother went to Elisha, the conduit of her blessing, and told him what had happened. She insisted that he come home with her.

Even in her sadness, she had unshakeable hope that Elisha and his God could do something about her son's death. She was right. With faith and hope she trusted Elisha's God and He brought her son back to life.

DAY 68

Cameron Gets Donuts

Dear children, let's not merely say that we love each other; let us show the truth by our actions.

1 John 3:18 NLT

Just five days before an out-of-state move, the COVID-19 quarantine was enforced. Eight-year-old Cameron was forced to say goodbye to his classmates in a quick few minutes as opposed to the big party the teacher had planned for the next day.

He got off the bus that same day only to hear that his farewell party with his soccer team had been canceled as well. He wouldn't get to say goodbye to any of his friends.

His mom took her devastated son to deal with disappointment the only way she knew would help...food. They went to a local donut shop where Cameron ordered an ice-cream cone with a side of two donuts. When he opened the donut bag, he found that the lady had given him six donuts instead of two. "Mom," he said, "You need to fix this!" Reluctantly, his mom went to pay for the extra donuts. But the kind lady refused her money. "I know he only asked for two," she said, "but he looked like he needed some cheering up."

And…there is *kindness*

With one simple gesture, this lady reminded Cameron that there are kind people in this world who pay attention to others. She gave him hope that eventually he wouldn't hurt so badly.

While disappointment ruled his day, a stranger had the power to turn his day around. She gave him a little bit of hope covered in sprinkles.

DAY 69

Keeping the Peace

"Thank God for your good sense! Bless you for keeping me from murder and from carrying out vengeance with my own hands."

1 Samuel 25:33 NLT

David's soldiers were tired and hungry. He knew that a wealthy man named Nabal lived nearby and he was harvesting crops and shearing sheep.

David and his army had protected some of Nabal's workers and flocks in the past. So, David expected Nabal to respond positively to David's servant's request for some food. David was wrong. Nabal was a crude, mean man. He sent David's servants away empty-handed after blasting them with rude comments.

David angrily gathered his soldiers and vowed that none of Nabal's men would even be alive by the next morning.

And...there is *intercession*

One of Nabal's servants ran to Abigail, Nabal's wife, and told her what had happened. He knew David was angry and that they were in big trouble.

Abigail sprang into action, gathering baskets of food. She set off to find David and actually met him on his way to kill her husband.

Abigail apologized for her husband's behavior and begged David not to kill him. She reminded him of the way he obeyed God and challenged him not to do evil now.

David listened to her. He even thanked her for stopping him from doing something wrong. Abigail took a chance and interceded. That made all the difference.

Fearless Compassion

Jesus reached out and touched him. "I am willing," he said. "Be healed!" And instantly the leprosy disappeared.

Matthew 8:3 NLT

When a person was stricken with leprosy in Jesus' time, it was debilitating, isolating, and an eventual death sentence. Not many people recovered. Leprosy was so contagious that its victims had to move away from family and friends to live in a place with only other leprosy patients. No more in-person contact, no pats on the back, handshakes, hugs...nothing. It was too dangerous. Perhaps you understand the lonely isolation, having experienced the COVID-19 quarantine.

Think about this—Jesus' reputation as one who could heal disease spread quickly. People followed Him everywhere, bringing their sick loved ones to Him, asking Him to heal them.

One leprosy victim heard that Jesus was nearby. He made his way to where Jesus was and cried out,

"You can heal me if You are willing." Remember… leprosy is very contagious. No one ever touched a person with leprosy.

And…there is *compassion*

Jesus' simple, tender response was, "I am willing." Jesus touched the man and he was healed; his life was restored. That's how much Jesus cares.

He is paying attention to you and what you're going through and His compassion is true and deep.

Friends and a Plan

His followers took him by night and lowered him in a basket through an opening in the wall.

Acts 9:25 NIV

Saul made it his life's mission to stop Jesus' followers from spreading the message of Jesus. He was ruthless at finding Jesus' followers and throwing them in prison. But, after Saul came to faith in Jesus he was a totally different man with a totally different mission. He even had a new name—Paul. He enthusiastically preached the message of Jesus—just as energetically as he had tried to stop the growth of Christianity.

News about the change in Paul spread, as did the power of his preaching. Jewish religious leaders who had counted on Paul's help in stopping Christianity now became angry at him. They actually plotted ways to kill him. Their spies constantly watched the city gates so they could attack him and kill him as he left town.

And...there is *help*

Paul's friends knew what the religious leaders were planning. God worked in their hearts and gave them courage and a plan.

Under the cover of night's darkness, they lowered Paul in a basket over the city wall so he could safely escape and continue preaching about Jesus in other towns. No problem is hopeless when God is involved. God calls on His people and they help.

Compassion like No Other

Jesus gave him back to his mother.

Luke 7:15 NLT

One day Jesus and His disciples came to the village of Nain. As usual, a large crowd followed Him. As they entered the town, they met a funeral procession on the way to bury a young man.

The dead man was the only son of a widow and she was understandably quite upset that her son had died. It was a challenge for a single woman in that culture to support herself.

This woman's son was her only hope for a future. Many friends walked along with the widow, weeping and grieving the death of her son. Jesus may have walked a few steps past them. Or perhaps He stopped as soon as He saw the grief-stricken mother.

And…there is *compassion*

Imagine Jesus' hand tenderly touching the woman's arm. Imagine His gentle but authoritative command, "Don't cry." Was He being unkind to say that? Of course not. Jesus knew what He was going to do.

Turning to the dead boy, he said, "Get up, young man." And the young man sat up…alive! Jesus gave the woman back her son.

Never doubt Jesus' care for you. He saw a broken-hearted mother and He had compassion. He has compassion for you, too.

DAY 73

Promises Kept

"I have seen Your salvation, which you have prepared for all people. He is a light to reveal God to the nations, and He is the glory of Your people Israel!"

Luke 2:30-32 NLT

Simeon was a devout man of God. Like many serious God-followers who knew the Scriptures, he was waiting with great anticipation for the Messiah to come. The Holy Spirit had actually promised Simeon that he would not die until he had seen the Messiah. He was getting older, but he believed that promise because he trusted God completely.

When Mary and Joseph brought the infant Jesus to the temple in Jerusalem to dedicate Him to God, the Spirit prompted Simeon to go to the temple that day. He saw Mary, Joseph and the Baby and God's Spirit spoke to his heart. "This Baby Boy is the Messiah I have promised."

And...there is *joy*

Imagine the explosion of joy in Simeon's heart as he took baby Jesus in his arms and praised God. Simeon had trusted God to keep His promises, regardless of how long he had to wait.

God did keep His promise. He always does. Simeon's trust was rewarded when he held Jesus in his arms and joy flooded his heart.

He could die a happy man now, having seen the Messiah face-to-face.

Lori vs. Fractions

Dear friends, let us continue to love one another, for love comes from God. Anyone who loves is a child of God and knows God.

1 John 4:7 NLT

Lori vs. fractions. No matter how hard she tried, Lori could not wrap her brain around fractions. Finally, she gave in and went to the person who knew everything...her dad.

The pattern developed—each night Dad came home from work, ate dinner, then the two of them sat at the kitchen table for hours, painfully going through every fraction-themed math equation. Every night ended the same way—with Lori's tears and shouting.

And...there is *love*

Lori and her dad were working as hard as they individually could but the only math happening was a growing division between the two of them.

That's when Lori's dad made a decision: "Lori, I love you too much to expect an A in math." Lori sat there stunned. Dad had spent so much time trying to help her understand fractions because it came so easily to him. "If you earn a D in math, I will be proud of you because I know you've worked very hard at this."

Just like that, the pressure was off. Dad knew that a relationship with his daughter far outweighed a letter grade. Considering all he knew as a student, teacher and parent...he chose love.

Giving Lori permission to work hard and still not achieve what he could achieve was one of the greatest lessons he taught her.

DAY 75

The Courage of Obedience

God was good to the midwives, and the Israelites continued to multiply, growing more and more powerful.

Exodus 1:20 NLT

Pharaoh, the king of Egypt, captured the entire nation of Israel and made slaves of every person. It was a difficult life. The Egyptians were tough taskmasters and were brutal to the slaves.

Then Pharaoh became nervous because the Hebrews kept having babies. There were more and more Hebrews! He was nervous that there would soon be so many Hebrews that they could rebel. He didn't want to lose his slaves and he didn't want the Hebrews to be more powerful than he was. So, Pharaoh ordered the Hebrew midwives who helped with the births of the Hebrew babies to kill all the baby boys born. The Hebrew baby girls could live.

And...there is *courage*

Two of the Hebrew midwives, Shiphrah and Puah, secretly refused to obey Pharaoh. They let the baby girls *and* the baby boys live. They were risking their own lives by doing this but they knew that what Pharaoh was asking was wrong.

When questioned by Pharaoh, they answered, "The Hebrew women deliver the babies so quickly that the births are done before we can get there." God protected the two women and even rewarded them by giving them their own families.

God rewards the courage of obedience.

DAY 76

Faith Rewarded

"Dear woman," Jesus said to her, "your faith is great. Your request is granted." And her daughter was instantly healed.

Matthew 15:28 NLT

What will you do for someone you love? Think about the woman who stopped Jesus and asked Him to heal her daughter who was possessed by a demon. Jesus didn't respond to her right away. But, evidently, she kept asking until Jesus' disciples became annoyed with this Gentile who was bothering Him.

They told Jesus to send her away. Did the woman give up and leave? No, she kept asking until Jesus told her that He had come to help the Jews, not the Gentiles. Did the worried mother finally give up and leave then?

And…there is *reward*

No, she bravely reminded Jesus that even dogs get to eat the crumbs that are dropped from the table. She felt she deserved His help and she believed Jesus could cast the demon out of her daughter.

Jesus was touched by her courage, persistence and faith and He made the demon immediately leave her daughter.

Never be afraid to ask Jesus for what you want. He will always do what's best. He hears your heart's cry and He will answer.

DAY 77

It Wasn't Over!

Then Jesus told him, "Follow Me."

John 21:19 NLT

No one can say that Peter did things halfway. When Peter committed to something, he committed 200%. Think about when Jesus told the disciples that they would all desert him when the going got tough. Peter's response was, "*Not me*! I'm with You no matter what, Jesus!"

A few short hours later, Peter had denied even knowing Jesus—not once or twice, but *three* times. That's exactly what Jesus had said would happen.

Peter had been "all in" about never deserting Jesus, but then he was "all in" about denying he even knew Jesus.

The great thing about this is that the story wasn't over. Peter's life of service to Jesus didn't end with those three denials.

Jesus forgave him and later told Peter to follow Him. He offered new opportunities for Peter to be involved in growing the kingdom.

Once again, Peter was "all in" with serving God. He took those opportunities and did some amazing things with God and that was made possible by Jesus' forgiveness.

DAY 78

Lot Hesitates

When Lot still hesitated, the angels seized his hand and the hands of his wife and two daughters and rushed them to safety outside the city, for the LORD *was merciful.*

Genesis 19:16 NLT

Lot saw two angels outside Sodom's city gate. He immediately bowed his face to the ground and insisted that they come to his home. He prepared a feast for them. Before they could lie down to rest, the men of Sodom surrounded his house. They shouted for him to send his guests out. They didn't have good intentions.

The situation got so bad that Lot actually offered to send out his virgin daughters instead of the angels. But the angels saw how evil the men of Sodom were. They struck the entire crowd with blindness and told Lot to grab his family and run.

And...there is *grace*

In the span of one evening, Lot hosted angels, offered to sacrifice his daughters and was told to flee his home before the wrath of God fell on the town. His response was...hesitation. It was like he needed a moment to wrap his head around what had happened and what was about to happen.

The angels knew there was no time for hesitation. They grabbed Lot's hand and led him outside the city. An understandably human moment from Lot turned into a lifesaving moment of grace from God.

Fear turned into pause turned into grace. Lot's pause gave space for God's grace.

DAY 79

Life with Jesus Means Hope

Jesus told her, "I am the resurrection and the life. Anyone who believes in Me will live, even after dying. Everyone who lives in Me and believes in Me will never ever die. Do you believe this, Martha?"

John 11:25-26 NLT

Mary, Martha and Lazarus were good friends with Jesus. Apparently, Jesus often visited their home when He was in Bethany. When Lazarus got sick, his sisters sent for Jesus because they knew…they believed that Jesus could heal Lazarus and restore his health. But, Jesus didn't come for several days. By the time He did arrive, Lazarus was dead and had been buried four days.

Martha and Mary were heartbroken and confused as to why Jesus hadn't come. When He did arrive, Martha tearfully said, "I know my brother would still be alive if You had come."

And...there is eternity

The three siblings believed Jesus was the Messiah. They believed His message of hope, love and eternity. But, in their grief, Mary and Martha's faith stumbled a bit.

However, Jesus wasn't done. That's the great thing about life with Jesus—there's always an "and." He reminded the sisters that He is the Resurrection and the Life *and* life with Him is eternal!

DAY 80

Whatever God Wants

Mary responded, "I am the Lord's servant. May everything you have said about me come true." And then the angel left her.

Luke 1:38 NLT

By all accounts Mary was a young teen. She was engaged to be married to Joseph. Mary must have been a girl of good character, high standards and strong faith because...she was chosen to be the mother of Jesus.

No doubt it was frightening for Mary when the angel told her that she was going to have a baby. She knew she was a virgin and that her reputation could be ruined. She didn't know how Joseph would respond or even what her family would say. Would they believe an angel had come to her? Would they believe that she was pregnant with the Son of God? Would they believe she was chosen...or that she had "fallen"?

And...there is *submission*

It hardly took a moment before Mary said, "I'll do whatever God wants." Her faith in God was strong.

She believed He would be with her through whatever the future held. She was willing to do what He asked of her.

Mary's trust in God and desire to be of service to Him was stronger than any of her concerns or fears so she submitted to His will.

DAY 81

Brody Can't Walk

When I am afraid, I will put my trust in You.

Psalm 56:3 NLT

Two-year-old Brody was up all night crying in pain. Early the next morning, Brody sat on the floor while his mom called the doctor. As she reached for her phone, she noticed Brody scooting across the floor on his knees.

At the doctor's appointment, she mentioned this and within seconds the doctor was dictating instructions as he hurried her toward the hospital lab. "He has an infection in his hip. We need to find out if it is viral or bacterial. That will determine whether he will walk again."

And...there is *fear*

It takes moments of fear to appreciate the small things. Hearing that her son may possibly never walk again meant that Brody's mom prayed with each terrifying step as they left the hospital and awaited the diagnosis. She loved her son. She trusted God. Still she was anxious.

Late in the evening the doctor called with the lab results. All the anxious mom heard was, "He will walk again." That's all she needed to hear.

Of course, she knew that in the future she would grow weary of chasing those little feet around. But, in this moment, her fear melted away as she thanked God for strength and the power of prayer.

DAY 82

Faith in Motion

His mother told the servants, "Do whatever He tells you."

John 2:5 NLT

Jesus and His disciples were guests at a wedding—before His ministry had begun…before anyone knew who He was. Jesus' mother, Mary, was also a guest at this wedding.

Not much is known about Mary except that she was chosen by God to be the human mother of His Son. She was told some amazing things about her Son from the angel Gabriel and by Simeon and Anna in the temple.

Nothing is written about Jesus from the time He was 12 years old until He was 30. But now, they are both guests at this wedding and Mary notices that the host is about to run out of wine. It would be embarrassing for him to be unable to serve his guests. She wants to help.

And...there is a *miracle*

Mary tells Jesus about the problem because she knows He can help. She believes He has the power to solve the problem.

Mary's faith in Jesus sets the stage for His first public miracle—turning water into wine—and sets in motion all that the Father has planned for Him as He begins His ministry, which means He set in motion all that He has planned for us!

DAY 83

The Power of Prayer

To Him who is able to do immeasurably more than all we ask or imagine, according to His power that is at work within us, to Him be glory in the church and in Christ Jesus throughout all generations, for ever and ever! Amen.

Ephesians 3:20-21 NIV

Peter was in prison for no other reason than King Herod wanted to please the Jews who were enemies of Jesus. He was winning their favor by persecuting and killing believers.

Peter was chained and guarded by four squads of four soldiers each.

Herod wanted to be sure he didn't escape and that there was no chance of him being rescued. He planned to bring Peter to trial after the Feast of Unleavened Bread. It would not be a fair trial. Peter's doom was set.

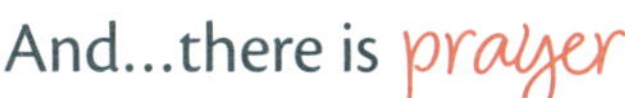

King Herod thought he had things under control. He believed that no one could stand against him. But he didn't know about the power of prayer.

Peter's friends gathered in a secret place and called on God to rescue their friend. God did! He broke Peter's chains. He blinded the guards. He sent an angel to lead Peter safely out of prison to freedom!

God's people prayed. God answered.

DAY 84

Jude Visits Heaven

This is how God loved the world: He gave His one and only Son, so that everyone who believes in Him will not perish but have eternal life.

John 3:16 NLT

Jude was four years old when his great-grandmother passed away. They saw each other often since she lived with Jude's grandparents who babysat him most days. Jude usually brought her breakfast and greeted her with a "Morning, Super G" (his nickname for her).

When she died, Jude and his family drove to Missouri to bury her next to Great-Grandpa. As they left the hotel for the funeral, Jude asked where they were going.

His mom responded, "We're going to see Super G one last time." As they pulled into the parking lot of the funeral home, Jude's eyes lit up and he exclaimed, "Is this heaven?"

And...there is *belief*

Only a four-year-old would confuse a parking lot in small-town Missouri for heaven. The beauty of this misunderstanding is that Jude was less concerned about the look of heaven and more focused on the existence of heaven.

He knew Super G was going there. He knew that God would be there. All of that was enough for him to look past the blustery February morning and crumbling parking lot. His focus was on the existence of heaven and the loved ones who were already there.

DAY 85

A Community of Prayer

"If two of you agree here on earth concerning anything you ask, My Father in heaven will do it for you. For where two or three gather together as My followers, I am there among them."

Matthew 18:19-20 NLT

Esther became queen through unusual (not actually good) circumstances. Perhaps she didn't even want to be queen. However, God put her in that place for a certain time and a certain purpose...to save the Jewish people...her people. When Haman threatened to kill all the Jews, Queen Esther was in the position to save them. It was risky. It was dangerous. She had to go before the king without being summoned. He could have her killed for that. However, she knew she had to do it.

Her plan was to invite the king and Haman to dinner where she would reveal Haman's plan and beg for her life and those of her people. But before the dinner she had a plan.

And...there is *prayer*

She asked her relative, Mordecai to have the Jewish people pray for her. She knew she needed their prayer support and the strength and courage that would give her. She prayed. They prayed.

She revealed Haman's plan and the king stopped it. The Jews were saved!

A community of prayer has power!

DAY 86

Facing Temptation

The temptations in your life are no different from what others experience. And God is faithful. He will not allow the temptation to be more than you can stand. When you are tempted, He will show you a way out so that you can endure.

1 Corinthians 10:13 NLT

Why? Why? Why? Why is it so hard to resist temptation? Giving in to temptation starts with a little thing. It seems rather innocent—no big deal—but then it grows into something a little bigger, then a little bigger still. It happens so slowly that you barely even notice that you are now giving in to the temptation to do things you know you shouldn't.

You can be determined to fight, to resist, to stay strong. But, the giving in happens way too often.

And...there is *understanding*

Jesus knows what you're going through. He battled Satan's sneaky temptations, too. He knows what you're feeling. He knows how difficult it is to push Satan away so He doesn't condemn you for the struggle.

But, you know what? Jesus resisted Satan. He stood strong against temptation...*and*...He will help you do the same. Cry out for His strength. Cry out for His wisdom and discernment. Cry out for His help. He will give it.

DAY 87

Following Jesus

He said to them, "Follow Me, and I will make you fishers of men."

Matthew 4:19 ESV

One thing in life that's constant is change. Things are always changing. Relationships beginning or ending, careers evolving or ending, aging, changes in family status, financial strains… any or all of these changes may affect your feelings about how you spend your days and what your purpose in life is.

Responsibilities have been taken away and what you felt your strength was seems to no longer be needed. How do you spend your days now? Where do you find your purpose, identity and value?

And...there is *purpose*

Remember when Jesus called His disciples to follow Him? None of the twelve were powerful leaders. They were fishermen and tax collectors...men who worked hard for a living.

When Jesus called them, they left their careers, income, family and yes, purpose behind. But He didn't leave them wondering what life held. He told them their new purpose.

He told them that from now on they would be fishing for men—winning souls to God. He has a purpose for you, too...every change in life is part of the plan.

DAY 88

Standing Strong

At the end of the ten days, Daniel and his three friends looked healthier and better nourished than the young men who had been eating the food assigned by the king.

Daniel 1:15 NLT

Daniel and his three friends were taken captive by the king of Babylon. Because of their strength and good health the four boys were placed in a special training program for the king's royal service.

They had the privilege of eating food and wine from the king's own kitchen. No doubt that was better rations than the other slaves enjoyed. However, Daniel didn't want to eat the king's food. He knew it would defile him.

It was important to Daniel that he honor God. He asked that he and his friends be given only vegetables and water.

The guard was understandably frightened that he would be punished if the four boys weren't as healthy as the other boys. Daniel asked for a ten-day test.

And...there is *reward*

Ten days of only vegetables and water while other boys in the training program had rich foods and fine wines and...Daniel and his friends were healthier and stronger than all the others.

God honored Daniel and his friends for honoring Him. Make God more important than anything or anyone else in your life. He will reward your obedience in ways that will amaze you.

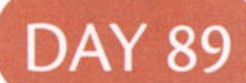

Paul and Silas in Prison

Around midnight Paul and Silas were praying and singing hymns to God, and the other prisoners were listening.

Acts 16:25 NLT

Paul and Silas were locked in the innermost part of the prison. Their crime? They freed a young woman from the demon that was possessing her. The men who owned her and made money from her were not happy.

Paul and Silas didn't get angry or bitter. In fact, around midnight they were locked in prison, praying and singing praises to God. The other prisoners were listening to them.

Suddenly there was a powerful earthquake, chains fell off prisoners, doors popped open. All the prisoners could escape! The jail guard drew his sword to kill himself rather than be killed because the prisoners escaped. But none of the prisoners left. Paul and Silas kept them all there.

And...there is *witness*

The jailer was amazed that all the prisoners were still there. He was impressed by Paul and Silas's testimonies of faith. "What must I do to be saved?" he asked. The jailer and all his family were saved because of this experience.

Give witness to your faith by standing strong in difficult times...sharing your faith whenever you can...being positive when things are hard.

Peace in a Storm

As evening came, Jesus said to His disciples, "Let's cross to the other side of the lake."

Mark 4:35 NLT

Jesus had just finished a marathon teaching session. He told many parables of farmers sowing seeds and lamps that needed to shine bright and how a tiny mustard seed could grow into a giant tree. He wanted the people to understand how faith in God could grow stronger and stronger.

As night fell, a very tired Jesus and His disciples got into a boat to cross the lake, leaving the crowds behind. All was fine until a big storm blew up and the disciples became terrified that their boat would sink.

And...there is *peace*

The disciples were scared. Jesus was sleeping. Did He know what was happening? Of course, He is Jesus. When His friends woke Him, Jesus spoke only a few words and the storm simply stopped. Nothing is a match for His power. Not even the worst storm.

When trouble comes, cry out to Jesus and allow His peace to calm you. His presence is constant and His power is without equal.

About the Authors

Carolyn Larsen is a prolific and best-selling author and an experienced speaker with a God-given passion for ministering to women and children. She has spoken at conferences and retreats around the United States, Canada, and India. Carolyn has written over 50 books for children and adults. Her writing has won various awards. Carolyn lives in Wisconsin with her husband, Eric. They have three children and are proud grandparents.

Cori Cheek spent most of her adolescent and young adult life traveling nationally and internationally, performing with a creative arts worship team. She has since settled down in Virginia with her husband and three boys who hysterically and thoughtfully provide most of her writing material.